AFFIRMING CATHOLICISM

Jeffrey John

WHAT IS
AFFIRMING
CATHOLICISM?

DARTON·LONGMAN+TODD

JEFFREY JOHN is the Vicar of Holy Trinity, Eltham, and was formerly Dean of Divinity at Magdalen College, Oxford. He is a member of the national steering committee of Affirming Catholicism and series editor of these booklets. He is also the editor of Affirming Catholicism's conference books, *Living Tradition* and *Living the Mystery* (both DLT).

Published by Darton, Longman and Todd, 1 Spencer Court,
140–142 Wandsworth High Street, London SW18 4JJ
in association with Affirming Catholicism, St Mary-le-Bow,
Cheapside, London EC2V 6AU

ISBN 0–232–52145–X

The views expressed in this booklet are those of the
author and do not necessarily reflect any policy
of Affirming Catholicism.

Booklets designed by Bet Ayer, phototypeset by Intype, London
and printed by Halstan and Co Ltd, Amersham, Bucks

CONTENTS

Affirming Catholicism

Affirming Catholicism has never been, and is not intended to be, yet another 'party' within the Church of England or the Anglican Communion but rather a movement of encouragement and hope.

A group of lay people and clergy met together in 1990 to identify that authentic Catholic tradition within the Church which appeared to be under threat. Wider support was expressed at a public meeting on 9 June 1990 in London and at a residential conference in York in July 1991.

Since then Affirming Catholicism has been afforded charitable status. The following statement is extracted from the Trust Deed:

> It is the conviction of many that a respect for scholarship and free enquiry has been characteristic of the Church of England and of the Churches of the wider Anglican Communion from earliest times and is fully consistent with the status of those Churches as part of the Holy Catholic Church. It is desired to establish a charitable educational foundation which will be true both to those characteristics and to the Catholic tradition within Anglicanism ... The object of the foundation shall be the advancement of education in the doctrines and the historical development of the Church of England and the Churches of the wider Anglican Communion, as held by those professing to stand within the Catholic tradition.

In furtherance of these aims and objectives, Affirming Catholicism is producing this series of booklets. The series will encompass two sets of books: one set will attempt to present a clear, well-argued Catholic viewpoint on issues of debate facing the Church at any given time; the other set will cover traditional doctrinal themes. The editor of the series is Jeffrey John; the other titles in the series are listed at the back of this booklet.

To order these publications individually or on subscription, or for enquiries regarding the aims and activities of Affirming Catholicism write to:

The Secretary
Mainstream
St Mary-le-Bow
Cheapside
London EC2V 6AU

Tel: 0171–329 4070

Introduction

When I was seventeen I abandoned my Welsh Calvinist background and, following the lead of my older sister who had been educated at a local convent school, began taking instruction to become a Roman Catholic. One day during this period – it was August the fifteenth – I walked by chance into a church I did not know in a neighbouring town. High Mass had just begun for the feast of the Assumption of Our Lady. I supposed, naturally enough, that I had walked into a Roman Catholic church – though a rather nicer one than I had hitherto encountered, with a grander liturgy, better music and a decent sermon. There were all the usual accoutrements – confessional box, statues, lamps, incense and so on. The only perceptible differences were that the language of the liturgy was not quite the same, my co-worshippers were not Irish, and the place was altogether much more tasteful and middle-class than I had become used to. So I had doubts, and checked on the way out with one of the priests who stood at the door.

'This is a Catholic church, isn't it?' I asked.

'Of course it is,' he replied.

'Good,' said I, and explained that I was taking instruction with the convent chaplain to become a Catholic myself.

'Oh, you mean you're going to be a ROMAN Catholic,' he exclaimed. 'Don't be a silly bugger: come to tea tomorrow!'

Such was my introduction to Anglo-Catholicism, and I am grateful for it. My invitation to tea brought me the discovery that it was indeed possible to be a Catholic yet not a Roman Catholic. For me it was a welcome discovery, because attracted as I was by the glories of the Catholic faith, even at the age of seventeen I had serious doubts about Roman claims. An infallible Pope was particularly hard to swallow. I had read enough to know how shaky were the historical and doctrinal grounds on which the theory rested; and the notion of an unchallengeable leadership seemed to me potentially dangerous, and out of character with the Christ who calls us friends not slaves. Despite a developing devotion to Mary and the saints, I found the doctrine of her sinlessness and immaculate conception difficult too. If for Jesus to be sinless Mary had to be sinless too, why, I wondered, not St Ann, and all his forebears back to Eve? Reading the attempts to provide a theological justification for the doctrine, it was hard not to feel that there was something strange in the Roman attitude to sin and sex, almost as if sin were regarded as a sexually transmitted disease. Connected with this was the stance on contraception. At the time Paul VI, against expectation and, as it later emerged, against all theological advice, had just restated his opposition to birth control. I was scandalized by what I saw then, and still see now, as a cruelly irresponsible piece of dogma.

These difficulties – which are of course the standard Anglican ones – together with the more congenial social and intellectual atmosphere of the Anglican Church, won the day, though I spent almost a year hovering between the two possibilities. It was crucial that Anglicanism seemed to offer, along with all the riches I had discovered in the Catholic Christianity, a freedom of conscience and belief which seemed unavailable in Roman Catholicism or in the equally totalitarian form of Welsh Calvinism I had left behind. That freedom seems if anything more crucial now than it did then, because at least in the seventies one could still hope that Vatican II and a 'conciliar' or 'collegial' redefinition of infallibility might improve the situation. In fact something approaching the opposite has happened. The present papacy has unilaterally imposed conservative bishops on dioceses which used to be independent; thrown out others it has deemed too 'liberal'; unlicensed some of its very best theologians such as Küng, Schillebeeckx and Curran, and flooded the curia with conservative cardinals in an attempt to fix the papal succession. In ecumenical matters positions have hardened; the Vatican's official response to the ARCIC agreements, given before the Church of England's decision to ordain women priests, was profoundly discouraging, and suggested strongly that by contrast with the ARCIC model of reunion through 'convergence', the Vatican's only model of reunion remains one of capitulation to its own view. Finally, perhaps the most disturbing development of all has been the attempt to ban discussion of certain issues in the Church, notably the issue of ordaining women. Regimes which ban discussion usually do so in the unacknowledged suspicion that they cannot stand up to reasoned scrutiny.

This is why I remain happy with my decision, and also why many Roman Catholics who long for renewal and reform within their own Communion have welcomed and supported Affirming Catholicism as we wrestle, in our Anglican context, with the problems of remaining faithful to Catholic tradition while trying to face squarely the task of relating it to the present day. The affinity between Affirming Catholics on both sides of the Roman-Anglican fence struck me again recently when I was asked by a Roman Catholic publishing house to prepare an Anglican edition of a best-selling popular presentation of Roman Catholic teaching. The editing exercise was itself instructive. Most of the rewriting involved sections about church government and authority, the status of other denominations, the pattern of Christian initiation, and the doctrine of marriage. Other sections, for example on sacramental confession and devotion to the saints, needed some expansion for the sake of Anglicans unused to those practices. The result is, the publishers believe, a statement of firmly Anglican teaching which will be useful and acceptable at least to the 'middle to high' portion of the Anglican spectrum. But the most glowing appreciation came from a Roman Catholic reviewer:

> This is fascinating. You end up with a Catholicism without the Pope, which includes women priests and bishops, emphasizes the role of the laity, accepts the truth in other churches and faiths, talks sense about sex and marriage, and translates things like sacramental and Marian doctrine into terms you can understand. It's bloody wonderful! When can I join . . . ?

The enthusiasm of this reaction brought home to me how little we Anglicans, and Anglican Catholics in particular, have appreciated the treasures of our inheritance – by contrast with others who can still only pray for the advantages we possess. (The phrase 'Catholicism without the Pope' reminded me of Bishop Gore, who delighted to call Anglicanism just that, though he, like many successors in his tradition, might also have been happy with a reformed papacy such as that envisaged in the ARCIC documents.) The attractiveness of such a Catholicism, especially in the present climate, is clear; yet far too long Anglicans in general and Anglican Catholics in particular have failed to grasp how precious a gift is committed to our charge, and instead have been wallowing in self-doubt and cynicism. The present decline in Anglican Catholicism is blamed on the ordination of women priests, but the truth is that the vision had faltered and the decline had set in long before; the admission of women to the priesthood merely exposed incoherencies and weaknesses which had been destabilizing and corroding the movement for decades.

Affirming Catholicism began as an impatient reaction to this loss of nerve, and to the negative, ghetto mentality into which Anglo-Catholicism had sunk. It had to be made clear that Catholicism could move on, without being disloyal to its past – indeed, that it must to survive. In a memorable phrase of Richard Holloway's, we decided to pick the torch out of the ditch.

Affirming Catholicism exists to do two main things.

1. We affirm the Catholicity of Anglicanism

Most of the problems in Anglo-Catholicism have derived from the fact that so many of its clergy and laity have doubted the legitimacy of Anglicanism itself, had little regard for its distinctive traditions and ethos, and derived their spiritual leadership and authority from Rome – despite the fact that as long ago as 1898, Rome repudiated the validity of Anglican orders and sacraments. The movement almost from its inception has been undermined by the abiding question of whether we are 'the real thing'; and some have regarded themselves more or less explicitly as a Papal fifth column. There is no gainsaying that many have made a marvellous contribution nonetheless; but the incoherence of this position inevitably had a corrosive and inhibiting effect on the movement as a whole. Now that we have admitted women to the priesthood in advance of the rest of the Church, some Anglo-Catholics have concluded that mainstream Anglicanism has finally forfeited its claim to catholicity and become a 'sect'. It is therefore of primary importance that we affirm that the Anglican Communion remains part of Catholic Christendom in the fullest sense, possesses the Catholic scriptures, creeds, sacraments and ministry now as before, and is in no way inferior to other parts of Catholic Christendom in its autonomous authority to order its life.

2. We affirm and continue the Catholic Movement within Anglicanism

In affirming our Anglicanism we also affirm its plural nature as a gift and a mark of its catholicity, but we recognize too that important parts of our Catholic inheritance are still unknown or under-valued within our own Church. Through its own internal instabilities and introversion, especially in recent years, Anglican Catholicism has failed effectively to share the wealth of Catholic doctrine and spirituality with the rest of the Anglican Church. The cutting edge of teaching and evangelism has long since passed elsewhere, and there is now a serious risk of imbalance in the Anglican mix. We urgently need to show to those inside and outside the Church a life-affirming, world-affirming, incarnational Catholic faith; the healing power of all the sacraments, properly understood and celebrated; the transcendent beauty of good liturgical worship; the importance of personal growth through disciplined spirituality, confession, spiritual direction, the daily office and meditation; the help available in our own monastic tradition, which is still unknown to half the Church; a full understanding of the Communion of Saints in doctrine and devotion, and much more besides.

In short, there is everything still to be done to explain to those inside and outside the Church why a confident, Affirming, Anglican Catholicism is a 'bloody wonderful' way of salvation.

What follows expands on these two fundamental aims.

We affirm the Catholicity of Anglicanism

What does Catholic mean?

William Pickering, in his sociological survey of Anglo-Catholicism, mercilessly highlights the chaotic ambiguities into which Anglo-Catholics have been led by a shifting use of the word 'Catholic':

> In Anglo-Catholic terminology it is common to refer to one member of the Church of England as 'Catholic' and another as 'just Anglican'. Indeed, to this very day it is not unknown for someone to say, 'I'm not Anglican; I'm Anglo-Catholic'. It is clear from such statements that not all members can be called Catholic in the sense in which Anglo-Catholics use the word. Those who are Catholic are so by self-designation. The dilemma is this. The Church of England must be Catholic, since it adheres to the scriptures, the creeds and the ecclesiastical orders of bishops, priests and deacons created by apostolic succession. Hence the Church is Catholic and all members must therefore be Catholic. Yet not all are Catholic! Numerically most are just 'ordinary C. of E. people!' What kind of Catholicism is it when in the one Church some are held to be Catholic and some are not? . . . To make matters more complicated, there are held to be degrees of Catholicism amongst Anglo-Catholics. Thus, one person is 'fairly Catholic' and another is 'very Catholic'. Anglo-Catholics actually disagree amongst themselves as to who among them is 'truly' Catholic and who is not.[1]

Affirming Catholics too have been accused of using the word Catholic to mean what we like. So what does it mean? It clearly does not necessarily mean Roman Catholic, as my first encounter with Anglo-Catholicism taught me. People of course use the word loosely in this way all the time, but it might be helpful if they did not, because Rome certainly does not hold a monopoly of Catholic faith. The reality is much more complex. Catholic is a slippery word, so I will try to be precise. The word is used in at least five ways, in addition to its misuse as shorthand for 'Roman Catholic':

1 Catholic comes from two Greek words meaning literally 'according to the whole'. Its original, basic and truest meaning is therefore something like 'universal', or 'all-embracing'. When the Church Fathers spoke of the Catholic Church they meant the whole Church, and the Catholic faith meant the faith held by all Christian people. In St Vincent of Lerins' famous dictum, the Catholic faith was *quod ubique, quod semper, quod ab omnibus creditum est* – 'that which has been believed everywhere, always, and by everybody'.

2 The second meaning derives from the first. Catholic came to mean 'the

true, right, correct Church' or 'the true, right, correct faith', as opposed to heretical or schismatic groups and faiths which were excluded by the test of 'universality'. (We have to note however that from the beginning there were always dissenting groups still calling themselves Christians, and so St Vincent's reference to a 'universal' faith was in fact only ever an appeal to a majority.)

3   After the Church suffered its first major split in 1054, neither side could truly claim to be 'the Catholic Church' in the proper and original sense of the word, since the Church was manifestly no longer whole. The eastern part of the Church, having rejected the authority of Rome, referred to itself as the Orthodox Church (literally the 'right-teaching' Church). The Western Church, however, continued to call itself the Catholic Church, believing, as it still officially does, that in some mysterious and unspecified way the whole Church continues to 'subsist' within it. In effect, however, it was at this point that Catholic began to be used to mean 'Roman Catholic'.

4   After the Reformation, certain churches, most notably the Anglican and Old Catholic churches, sometimes used the word Catholic to denote their possession of a historical and continuous tradition of faith and practice, centring on the claim to have preserved the historic episcopate. In Tractarian and Anglo-Catholic theology certain churches – Roman, Orthodox, Anglican, Old Catholic and one or two others – have been regarded as 'Catholic' churches, as opposed to those who at the Reformation did not preserve the order of bishops, priests and deacons in episcopal succession. (This view is often called the 'Branch Theory', implying that the 'tree' of the Catholic Church had forked, as it were, into three or more branches, but each still carried the sap of apostolic authority through the succession of bishops.) Both Laudian and Victorian High Church theologians argued that the Church of England, as the heir and successor of the pre-Reformation Church, was 'the Catholic Church of England', and some provinces of the Anglican Communion, notably in Japan and China, also called themselves 'The Holy Catholic Church' in that particular land. This usage could also carry the further implication that by purifying itself of Roman accretions and supposedly returning to the ancient faith of undivided Christendom, Anglicanism could actually be seen as 'more Catholic' than Roman Catholicism!

5   The term Catholic is frequently applied piecemeal to particular doctrines or practices which derive from the pre-Reformation period, or which are held in common with the Roman and Orthodox churches. Many of these doctrines and practices were reintroduced or re-emphasized in Anglicanism by the Tractarians and Anglo-Catholics in the last century. So one might speak of 'the Catholic doctrine of the Eucharist', 'the Catholic veneration of

saints', 'the Catholic understanding of priesthood', again without specific reference to Roman Catholicism.

Which kind of Catholicism are we affirming?
The first thing to underline is that no church (and certainly no group within a church) can claim for itself the title 'Catholic' in the first and truest sense given above, because in the divided state of Christendom no church is truly whole and universal. As William Temple is said to have remarked, 'I believe in the Holy Catholic Church and sincerely regret that it does not at present exist'. The Roman Church continues to claim that the whole Church 'subsists' within it, but it is hard to find meaning in the claim, especially since it now clearly recognizes, since Vatican II, the existence of other Christians who are members by faith and baptism of Christ's Body. In his booklet in this series entitled *Is the Anglican Church Catholic?* Vincent Strudwick points out that real catholicity can only ever reside in a reunited Church.² Catholicity is not something lost or possessed, it is something still to be achieved. John Habgood also writes in an essay on the catholicity of Anglicanism:

> True catholicity belongs as much to the future as to the past. It entails the creative development of tradition as well as humble respect for it.³

So in the first place, as Affirming Catholics, like all responsible Christians, *we affirm our hope for a truly Catholic, visibly united Church and our willingness to work for it.*

But how is this to be done? Clearly only by holding to agreed sources of authority which keep us centred on Christ and can serve as a basis for unity. This leads us into the second and third meanings of the word 'Catholic'. How do we know that the Church remains in possession of the truth, and faithfulness to the Gospel? What sources provide it, and what authorities guard and proclaim it? The clearest and most succinct statement of Anglicanism's sources of authority, and the most widely endorsed throughout the Anglican Communion, is the 'Chicago-Lambeth Quadrilateral' of 1888. This statement set down four articles or markers of catholicity which the conference of Anglican bishops agreed should serve as such a basis in negotiations towards Christian reunion. They are:

1   The Holy Scriptures of the Old and New Testaments, as 'containing all things necessary to salvation', and as being the rule and ultimate standard of faith.

2   The Apostles' Creed, as the Baptismal Symbol; and the Nicene Creed, as the sufficient statement of the Christian Faith.

3   The two Sacraments ordained by Christ Himself – Baptism and the Supper

of the Lord – ministered with unfailing use of Christ's words of Institution, and of the elements ordained by Him.

4   The Historic Episcopate, locally adapted in the methods of its adminis-tration to the varying needs of the nations and peoples called of God into the Unity of His Church.

The Quadrilateral is of course a minimum statement, but it enables us to affirm the catholicity of Anglicanism, in the sense that it possesses all the necessary markers of faithfulness to past revelation, and a safe framework for future development. On its basis we can affirm, in the words of the Ordinal, that the Anglican Church is 'a true part of the one, holy Catholic and Apostolic Church'. In this sense, as Pickering points out, it is therefore nonsense to hold that one group or individual in the Church is 'more Catholic' than any other. As Affirming Catholics, then, *we affirm the catholicity both of the Anglican Church and of all its members.* Of course we may still disagree with other members on individual points of faith and practice, but such diversity is a feature of all churches (even if Anglicanism may be said to specialize in it). The crucial thing is our fundamental confidence in the authority and catholicity of the Anglican doctrinal framework.

Nevertheless, we shall no doubt continue to speak in the fifth sense of 'Catholic Anglicans' as opposed to 'Evangelical Anglicans' or 'Liberal Angli-cans', just as we shall continue to speak of 'the Catholic doctrine' of the Eucharist and so on. To some this may seem to give the game away, but it does not. Anglicans in our tradition can legitimately and loyally see themselves as advocates within our own Communion of certain practices and beliefs which may still be more familiar to Roman Catholics and the Orthodox than the majority of our fellow Anglicans. There is more to be said about this later, but it would be a sad and bad thing for Anglicanism if the Anglo-Catholic mission to bring these insights to the surface and to enrich our tradition were to die. While hoping to have shed the self-doubt and neurosis of the past, *Affirming Catholicism affirms and continues to promote the warmth and wealth of Catholic tradition in our own Church.*

John Habgood, while lamenting the current state of Anglo-Catholicism, has written that nevertheless:

> the future lies with Catholicism. It must, because only Catholic tradition is rich enough and stable enough to be able to offer something distinctive to the world without being captured by the world. But it must be a Catholicism which is true to its highest vision, and hence broad enough, hospitable enough, rooted sufficiently in sacramental reality, confident enough in its inheritance to be able to do new things, diverse enough, and yet passionately enough concerned about unity, to be genuinely universal.[4]

That is the kind of Catholicism we affirm.

Catholicism and episcopacy
The fourth article of the Lambeth Quadrilateral is the one which causes most discussion and dissent. In the first place, it could seem to devalue totally the role and contribution of non-episcopal churches. David Hutt remarked at the 1993 Affirming Catholicism conference that Anglican Catholics need to repent of our consistently 'aloof and snooty' attitude to non-episcopal churches. Catholics in the General Synod were instrumental in the Church of England's rejection of the Anglican-Methodist unity scheme in 1972, and Anglo-Catholics in general have routinely opposed local or national ecumenical initiatives with Protestant churches. Part of the snootiness arises from the 'Branch' theory of the Catholic Church described above, which has played such a large part in Anglo-Catholic ecclesiology, and which has inevitably tended to suggest that those who were unattached to a 'branch' by bishops in apostolic succession were not truly part of the Church – and thus perhaps not truly Christian – at all. This view was often expressed by reference to Cyprian's adage, *ubi episcopus ibi ecclesia* – 'where the bishop is, there is the Church' – with the implication, 'where there is no bishop, there is no Church'.

The deprecation of non-episcopal churches is only one element in the traditional – and especially the more popular – Anglo-Catholic approach to episcopacy which needs correcting. The nineteenth-century ecclesiologists' preoccupation with the mechanical, tactile aspect of episcopal 'laying on of hands' led to the ludicrous proliferation of 'episcopi vagantes', eccentric bishops who were 'validly' ordained in the technical sense, but in communion only with tiny groups or with no one but themselves. Nor was it properly recognized that an 'unbroken' succession of bishops, leading ultimately back to the apostles and so to the Lord Himself, while an attractive idea, was most unlikely to correspond to historical fact. (It was a memorable Anglo-Catholic, Arthur Couratin, who liked to point out that the transfer of authority in the Church 'had more to do with bums on thrones than hands on heads'.) The pattern of the threefold ministry of bishop, priest and deacon, and the concept of apostolic succession, while a legitimate development from patterns and concepts of ministry present in the New Testament, can hardly be said to be firmly grounded in it. The assertion in the Preface to the Ordinal of the Book of Common Prayer that 'from the Apostles' time there have been these three Orders of Ministers in Christ's Church: Bishops, Priests and Deacons' is true but misleading. The threefold order was developed and systematized into a universal pattern only in the second century, in face of the Church's urgent need to guard its own integrity against the multiplication of endlessly fragmenting Gnostic sects. As such it proved extremely effective; and it is fair to point out that churches which have preserved the episcopal system have proved far lass fissiparous than those which have not. But it is important not to claim too much.

There is an old argument about whether episcopacy is 'of the *esse*' or 'of the *bene esse*' of the Church, i.e. whether it is essential for a church to be a true church at all (of the *esse*) or whether it is simply good for the 'wellbeing' of a church (of the *bene esse*). To argue that it is 'of the *esse*' of the Church effectively 'unchurches' all members of non-episcopal churches, and that is a wildly unreasonable view which was repudiated by the Lambeth Conference as long ago as 1920. It has also effectively been repudiated by the Roman Church, which since Vatican ii accepts that all those who have been duly baptized in the name of the Trinity, in whatever church, Roman or non-Roman, episcopal or non-episcopal, are nevertheless: 'incorporated into Christ. They therefore have the right to be called Christians, and with good reason are accepted as brothers by the children of the Catholic Church'.[5] The same document clearly recognizes baptism as the basis of Christian unity: baptism constitutes the sacramental bond of unity existing among all who through it are reborn'.[6] Of course, the others remain out of full communion with the Roman Catholic Church, and the Vatican statements carefully avoid any use of a term such as 'invisible Church' to explain how these separated brethren can be fully members of Christ's Body yet not Roman Catholics. Nevertheless it is clear that some such concept of an 'invisible' Church larger than the borders of the institutional Roman or episcopal churches must be operating here – the Church which is the mystical Body of Christ into which all are incorporated by baptism.

This limited but positive development in the Roman attitude to other churches has helped crystallize contemporary Anglican ideas about the nature of the Church. Recent work by Anglican ecclesiologists – notably Stephen Sykes and Paul Avis – has lamented the lack of a coherent theology of the Church in Anglicanism and argued strongly for the necessity of grounding such a theology more clearly in baptism.[7] It is baptism, not episcopacy which sets the limits of the Church; and for all its guarded language, even the Vatican accepts as much. Clearly then, we cannot argue that episcopacy is of the *esse* of the Church. Nevertheless, to say it is of the *bene esse* means more than that it is simply the best practical way of managing Church affairs and minimizing the risk of divisions. It might be best to say, with Hugh Montefiore, that episcopacy is of the *plene esse* of the Church – 'of the fullness'. While accepting that non-episcopal bodies are fully part of Christ's Church through faith and baptism, that their sacraments are efficacious means of grace, and that they frequently show clearer marks of the Church in terms of holiness and fellowship than does the Anglican Church, he has argued that in episcopacy Anglicans possess a non-negotiable sacramental gift which we have to offer to the whole Church:

The historic episcopate is a matter not only of pastoral but of theological importance. It provides the full embodiment of the Gospel in church order. It does this
in two respects. Firstly, the historic episcopate provides the effectual sign of unity.
It embodies in church order the biblical proclamation that Christ's church is one.
Secondly it embodies in church order the principle of apostolicity. The episcopally
ordained ministry is both 'sent' to represent Christ to his Church, and is representative of the Church. It provides the guardianship of the Word and sacraments, of the
faith and the flock of Christ. The historic episcopate is thus an effectual sign of
the relation of Christ to his Church; for it manifests his authority within his Church.

The historic episcopate is therefore the outward means and pledge that Christ's
Church is one and apostolic. It proclaims that the real nature of the Church is
given by God, and serves to actualize what it proclaims. It is not, however, a mere
matter of the Church's outward form. The Church is sacramental, and its outward
structure embodies grace and spirit. The historic episcopate will be a fully expressive
and instrumental sign only in the future re-united Church of Christendom. But that
does not mean Anglicans can afford to undervalue it in the present.[8]

Paul Avis too notes that:

> Anglicanism could not compromise on episcopacy as a principle of structural union,
> because the bishop is the *effective* symbol of unity, but in its right mind it could
> never dismiss the sacraments of non-episcopal communions as no sacraments, their
> ministers as no ministers, and their churches as no churches, as the more extreme
> proponents of the apostolic paradigm did.[9]

Opinions will differ as to the extent to which recognition of baptism and
other marks of faithfulness to Christ and the Gospel in non-episcopal
churches should make intercommunion and mutual recognition of ministries
possible prior to structural union. The Porvoo Agreement drawn up in 1992
between the British and Irish Anglican Churches and the Nordic and Baltic
Lutheran Churches may suggest a way forward which remains faithful to
genuine principles of catholicity. These Lutheran churches, unlike the Church
of Sweden with which we are already in communion, did not clearly maintain
the apostolic succession unbroken at the Reformation, but otherwise differ
little in doctrine and order from the Swedish Church. The Statement begins
with the acknowledgement of 'one another's churches as churches belonging
to the One, Holy, Catholic and Apostolic Church of Jesus Christ', where the
word of God is preached and the sacraments administered on the basis of
sharing in the common confession of the apostolic faith. It also states:

> We acknowledge that one another's ordained ministries are given by God as instru-
> ments of his grace and as possessing not only the inward call of the Spirit but also
> Christ's commission through his whole Body, the Church.
> We acknowledge that personal, collegial and communal oversight (episkope) is
> embodied and exercised in all our churches in a variety of forms, in continuity of
> apostolic life, mission and ministry; We acknowledge that the episcopal office is

valued and maintained in all our churches as a visible sign expressing and serving the Church's unity and continuity in apostolic life, mission and ministry.

The last point is strengthened in an appendix to the Church of England's publication of the Statement, where John Halliburton, after a review of the participating churches' history and practice, finds it: 'quite clear that the intention of the rites of these churches is to continue and ordain to the ministry of pastoral and spiritual oversight which from apostolic times has been the task of the bishop', and that all the essential and traditional elements of a rite of episcopal ordination in the Western Church are present.[10] This seems therefore to be a case where literally all that separates us is doubt about the mechanical, tactile continuity of episcopal succession. The Statement accordingly proposes that the churches commit themselves to a mutual recognition of ministries and to invite one another's bishops 'normally to participate in the laying on of hands at the ordination of bishops as a sign of the unity and continuity of the Church'.

Predictably, the Agreement has already come under fire from some Anglican Catholics, on the grounds that there will be an 'anomalous' period of recognizing as true bishops those who have not been ordained in a definite tactile succession. This negative reaction once again seems to betray a sad lack of self-confidence and forward vision. The truth is that no episcopal succession in any church can be traced without periods of anomaly; that the Lutheran doctrine and understanding of episcopacy is indistinguishable from our own; and that the aim of the Agreement is to heal a breach by ultimately re-establishing the outward sign of succession in churches where it is now in doubt. The temporary 'anomaly' seems well worth tolerating for the sake of reconstituting episcopal succession as the visible principle of catholicity throughout the national churches of Northern Europe. To welcome this would be to affirm Catholicism in the truest sense.

The ordination of women

It is fair to say that a major impetus behind the start of Affirming Catholicism was a reaction against the assumption, still made in some quarters, that to be a Catholic Anglican means to be opposed to the ordination of women to the priesthood. It was perhaps less a response to the issue itself, than a reaction against the overwhelming negativity which the issue generated in Anglican Catholicism and its representative bodies. Affirming Catholicism has never defined itself as a movement in favour of the ordination of women priests. There are members and supporters of Affirming Catholicism who remain opposed to it, and others who remain genuinely undecided. Nevertheless it is fair to say that by far the numerical majority of the membership and the general ethos are strongly in favour.

We cannot do justice to the debate here,[11] but there are two main lines of argument against the ordination of women priests. The first, which is the view that the priest has to be male in order to symbolize Christ, and that Christ had to be male because maleness is somehow inherent in God, is very hard to sustain. In particular, it is difficult to find a way of following this line of argument which does not ultimately entail denying that women are truly made in the image of God at all. This is a view which is suggested by one or two Pauline verses, and which as been expressed by one or two Catholic theologians such as Augustine and Albert the Great, but which in general the church has thankfully been reluctant to draw. On the contrary, the whole Church acknowledges that in baptism men and women equally are identified with Christ and renewed in his image. Contrary to an opinion beloved of some Anglo-Catholic clergy, it is baptism, not ordination which makes each of us an *alter Christus*, 'another Christ'. By baptism both men and women already share in Christ's priesthood, through being incorporated in the Royal Priesthood of Christ himself. The ordained priesthood is different from the priesthood of all believers, but is not something to be understood in isolation from it. It is a particular focusing in one individual of the Priesthood of Christ which in another way he shares with us all, and logically femaleness should be no more a bar to the ordained priesthood than it is to the royal priesthood of the whole people of God through baptism. There is nothing here to jeopardize a fully Catholic understanding of the character of priesthood or of the sacraments.

However, the sticking point for most Catholics who are opposed is the second line of argument, the issue of ecclesial authority. To them such a unilateral 'tampering' with the ordained ministry seems to jeopardize the catholicity of Anglicanism – to saw the fourth leg, as it were, off the Lambeth Quadrilateral. On this view it might be OK for Anglicans to ordain women priests if the Pope and the Orthodox did so as well; but we can't do it on our own and yet still claim our bishops, priests and deacons are the same as theirs are.

The argument looks strong at first sight because clearly the ordination of women priests and bishops makes a big visible difference to the ordained ministry. But it is not clear why it should be thought to make a theological or ecclesiological difference. Ordaining women does not inherently threaten a Catholic understanding of order and authority. It does not mean abandoning the threefold ministry or even interrupting apostolic succession, but deciding to admit a different sort of person into it. That is a different thing: it is a second-order, not a first-order issue. In the case of the diaconate we made the same decision years ago, also unilaterally, but with very little anguish. Nor does the priesting of women alter our position *vis-à-vis* the rest of the Catholic Church. In the debates over the issue Anglican Catholics were consistently prone to gloss over the harsh fact that the Romans and most of the Orthodox did not recognize our orders anyway, and even if we had not ordained women it would probably still be a long time before they did. The Vatican's response to the ARCIC documents had already made that clear.

Although it is painful to think that this decision *may* postpone recognition and reunion still further, and although we must take the Pope's warnings on the subject seriously, we must take our Anglicanism seriously too. Though convinced we are fully members of Christ's one Holy Catholic and Apostolic Church, we are separated from Rome now on conscientious grounds, and have chosen to become or remain Anglicans precisely because there are certain freedoms and principles which we put first. It makes no sense for Anglican Catholics to appeal to outside 'authority' on this issue, when that 'authority' already denies the validity of our own priesthood. Much as we may long for reunion and intercommunion, they cannot be pursued at *any* cost. Points of ecumenical pragmatism must not override points of principle, otherwise why be an Anglican at all? Once we had decided it is right in itself to ordain women priests, and that it is not inconsistent with Catholic faith and order, we had a positive duty to get on with it. It is not an unCatholic move, but rather – as both Stephen Sykes and Vincent Strudwick put it – 'an act of eschatological obedience to the future Catholic Church'.

The ordination of women makes the Church more whole, more Catholic in the most fundamental sense, by including the whole of humanity in the ministry which represents God to us, and us to God. It is noteworthy that when the Old Catholic Church took the same step in 1989 of committing itself to the ordination of women to the priesthood, it did so precisely on these grounds of catholicity:

> We know ourselves to be called to a catholicity which excludes only everything which undermines the relationship of God to his people. Our confession of faith in the Creed, 'We believe in the One, Holy, Catholic and Apostolic Church' obliges us therefore no longer generally to limit the apostolic ministry to the masculine part of the body of the baptized.[12]

We must pray that the rest of the Catholic Church will also see it so sooner rather than later. It will not have been the first issue in which Anglicans have led and Rome followed.

We affirm and continue the Catholic Movement within Anglicanism

Teaching the Faith in a pluralist Church

Only once since becoming an Anglican have I suffered from the ailment known to Anglo-Catholics as 'Roman Fever'. It was shortly after I was ordained a priest, when I was asked to take over the chaplaincy of a hospital in my parish where the regular chaplain was sick. The most I could do was to go in a couple of mornings a week, taking the Blessed Sacrament with me for any patients who wanted to receive Communion. As I went around the wards patients would occasionally call me: 'Father, can I receive Communion?' or 'Father, can I make my confession?' Almost always they would turn out to be Roman Catholics. By contrast I would find myself practically begging Anglicans to receive Communion. Often they would react to the suggestion with complete surprise. Sometimes they would say astonishing things, such as 'Not today, thank you dear; I've got a bit of a headache.' And on one unforgettable occasion, 'Not now, Vicar: it might spoil my tea!'

It was funny, but it also hurt. I was newly ordained, wanting to give them the best I had to give, and the best I had to give was not understood or required, even by patients who were apparently practising Anglicans and who had asked to see the Chaplain. One telling response came from a lady who told me she had been a churchwarden: 'But how can I have Communion with only you and me here? There's not enough people to have Communion *with*' – an interesting example of exclusive emphasis on the 'horizontal' meaning of the sacrament. Things got worse when, later on, I was asked to do another stand-in chaplaincy at a home for terminally ill cancer patients. I was able, of course, to spend time with them and pray with them. But I was almost never able to give them what I knew they most needed and should have been able to receive. I wanted to give them the Last Rites. They needed nothing more desperately than the assurance of Jesus' tangible presence in Communion; the certainty of his loving forgiveness and acceptance in confession and absolution; the strengthening and healing of anointing. In the face of death, perhaps above all other times, we need the reassuring objectivity and physicality of the sacraments. It seemed to me then, and still seems to me now, a scandal that no one had ever given them the knowledge to be able to draw on those things; it is too late to give proper confirmation classes at a deathbed. Again this contrasted sharply with the

Roman Catholic patients, who knew precisely how to die – even the lapsed knew how to be reconciled – and who seemed to me greatly blessed by comparison with their fellow patients.

'Moderate' Catholic Anglicans sometimes like to imagine that the Catholic movement in the Church of England has achieved most of its aims. The Parish Eucharist is now the norm, many churches and most cathedrals reserve the Sacrament, various feasts and ceremonies have been added to the ASB, and lots of priests wear vestments and are called 'Father'. Much of this however is window-dressing. Many externals of Catholic practice may have trickled down; but solid Catholic doctrine, devotion and discipline have to be taught and exemplified. The abiding pain of being a Catholic-minded priest in the Anglican Church is knowing that no matter how well you educate your congregation, outside your own patch there is no consensus of teaching and practice in the Church on which to rely. In most parts of this country Anglican Catholicism has been and remains essentially eclectic and con-gregationalist – in a sense, as has already been said, the opposite of what 'Catholic' should mean. My experience with the lady who didn't want to spoil her tea was depressing enough. It is even worse to know that one's own parishioners may one day have to cope with clergy whose sacramental theology is equally minimal.

But we do not despair. Catholic-minded Anglicans have always had to accept that as well as a mission to the world we have a mission to our own church. But it is not a mission that could ever be accomplished by despising our own church and half-wishing ourselves elsewhere. This is one of the reasons why Affirming Catholicism has strongly resisted seeing itself as another party in the Church. We are called to be 'a leaven to the lump . . . until all is leavened'. Our foundation statement describes us as 'a movement of encouragement and hope . . . for the advancement of education in Catholic doctrine within the Anglican Communion'. In the extraordinary mix of the community to which God has called us, we are asked to share with the rest the wealth of our own inheritance. There is a real hunger for what we have to offer, it only we will take the trouble to explain and communicate it.

Forgive yet more autobiography, but I have found this to be true both as a parish priest and as a university chaplain. In terms of teaching the faith in a pluralist church, my experience as a chaplain was particularly instructive. Like the majority of Anglican university chaplains, I frequently bemoaned the fact that students seemed almost never to come from Anglo-Catholic or middle-of-the-road parishes, or if they did, they had stopped worshipping by the time they became students. Practising Christian students were overwhelm-ingly Evangelical, and often of a very naive sort. But it also became clear to me from regularly attending Christian Union meetings and Bible studies (frequently biting my lip) that a high proportion were unhappy in their

Evangelicalism, especially as they grew older and more complicated. It did not surprise me to hear from the Vicar of the biggest of the local Evangelical churches that a survey had shown that more than half his church's student worshippers ceased to practise after leaving Oxford. It seemed that, for these young people at least, Evangelicalism was the only possible way in to faith, but not a very effective means of growing up in it. While still at College most Evangelicals tended to become increasingly doubtful about a too simplistic and literal approach to scripture and theology, and often felt strait-jacketed by a too rigid approach to personal and sexual ethics. Stock Evangelical positions with regard to other faiths, the fate of non-believers, the meaning of the cross and resurrection, faith and works, personal morality, heaven and hell, increasingly failed to convince. After leaving, they sometimes found it hard to find the same kind of emotive worship and preaching, or had grown tired of it. Not possessing a doctrine of the Church and sacraments, and having been taught, implicitly or explicitly, to regard non-Evangelical churches as 'unsound' or simply 'dead', there was no other recourse.

I found however that by pointing out this likely pattern of events in advance, and suggesting the need of a more grown-up faith for spiritual survival, most Evangelical students were more than willing to take large doses of Catholic teaching and practice on board. It needed some care. It could only be done by making it very clear that I was serious about being a Christian myself. (That may seem obvious, but in my observation clergy in higher education are frequently so embarrassed and apologetic about their role that they make it easy for Evangelicals and everyone else to conclude they actually believe nothing; sometimes of course that is the case). It depended partly too on being willing to talk the same language (being raised as a nonconformist has its uses); on being able to pray without using a book; on preaching and teaching with some energy and enthusiasm; on rooting doctrine in scripture; and on being willing to spend time with individuals in their struggle to develop a viable faith. Given those things, I have never found such fertile ground for sowing Catholic seed. Perhaps because I had done it myself, to move from Evangelicalism to Catholicism came to seem the natural progression.

This will sound insufferably patronizing to Evangelicals, but I do not mean to be. In the first place, my experience relates almost exclusively to young Evangelicals, often new to faith. In the second, I could only be complacent about Catholics in the Church if I believed we were doing God's work more effectively than Evangelicals, and that is plainly not the case. Catholics ought to be acutely aware how much we have to learn from Evangelicals, both spiritually and practically. Evangelicalism in the Church today has a freshness and energy long since disappeared from Anglo-Catholicism. It has an air of sincere striving for truth, which is miles away from the cynicism and seediness which so often deface Anglo-Catholicism. It has a seriousness about scripture, however blinkered it may sometimes be, that we desperately need to recapture. It makes itself easily accessible to outsiders, and welcomes them in, by caring about effective and powerful communication in church and in the media. It has developed systematic programmes for training and educating children, young people and adults, which are unrivalled in the rest of Church. It has, above all and by definition, a real desire and longing to bring souls to Christ.

A healthy Catholicism, also by definition, must *include* all these things, because it is about the *whole* faith. As Archbishop Carey reminded us at the first Affirming Catholicism conference in 1991, the opposite of Catholic is not Protestant but sectarian.[13] A whole Catholicism is able to affirm all true Evangelical Christian insights and instincts, and will not be truly Catholic until it does. I have observed that it seems a natural progression for Evangelicals, given a chance, to turn into Catholics, even if they still call themselves Evangelicals (there are several bishops in this category). I was not surprised to learn recently that the majority of postulants and novices in our Anglican religious communities come from Evangelical churches. The Lord is doing something new and wonderful in this way, and we can help. But we also need Catholics to be prepared to grow in the other direction, to be more willing to affirm Evangelical seriousness and sincerity, good practice and communication, systematic teaching, and zeal to share the faith with others. To have any value, comprehensiveness in the Church must mean more than the polite tolerance of disagreement: we need mutual comprehension too. It ought to be a major feature of Anglicanism that this cross-fertilization of traditions takes place to such an extent that the divisions ultimately blur – 'till all is leavened' – because we can all share in the fullness of Christ's gifts. The rich potential for this exchange is one of Anglicanism's strongest claims to catholicity in the truest sense, and there is everything to be gained from pursuing it. We have stayed far too long in our hermetically sealed compartments.

What have we got to offer?
Returning to ministry in a suburban parish, I have not found less of a hunger to be taught the Catholic faith, but more.

There is a hunger for the teaching of basic doctrine, which is most conspicuously lacking in the middle-of-the-road to Catholic range of parishes. What does salvation mean? What happens when we die? Why does the cross make a difference? Did Jesus really do miracles? What is the point of the doctrine of the Trinity? What is the meaning of almost any line of the Creed? Most of these things have not been systematically and effectively taught in parishes. Many parishioners who are highly sophisticated in their own jobs and education have never advanced beyond Sunday school in their grasp of the Christian faith. Most in my observation are very uncomfortable with their ignorance, want to change it, and will usually respond warmly to any serious effort to supply the teaching they need. Catholic preaching is notoriously in need of revival. Sermons are often scandalously bad – a repeatedly wasted opportunity – with far too little demand and expectation in our own tradition that they should be otherwise. Children's groups and confirmation groups are still far too often conducted on *ad hoc*, amateur basis, and it is questionable how many Church schools give children a firm grounding in Christian faith and practice. Only Evangelicals and Roman Catholics seem to produce anything like a professional, integrated catechetical programme, with the training and teaching aids it requires to make it work.

There is a hunger for Bible study, and it is wrong that so many Catholic parishes scarcely bother with it, as if the use of scripture belonged to an alien tradition. It is especially strange since Roman Catholicism after Vatican II has been re-emphasizing the centrality of scripture and strongly encouraging its study. By Bible study I do not mean only the 'devotional' kind which swaps personal experience, valuable though that can be. We also need Bible teachers in parishes who know something about critical Bible study, who can explain the background and editing behind the scriptures, how they grew, what kind of authority they have, and how they can help us now. I used to wonder, as a lecturer in New Testament theology, whether the notorious gap between academic theology and parish teaching could be bridged, and people allowed to see the questions and problems tackled by academic theologians without spreading alarm and despondency. Now I know it can. Christians want to be treated as grown ups, and allowed to know that sometimes there are no easy answers. Most welcome being let in on the discussion – and sometimes turn out to be sharper at it than the professionals.

There is a hunger for good and rich liturgical worship; but it is accompanied by a hunger for understanding it. So many 'middle-to-high' parishes across the country have bits of the ritual and paraphernalia of Catholic worship with little grasp of what it means in terms of doctrine and spiritual discipline. Liturgical clobber is used – incense, vestments, Reservation, holy water and what-not, without any explanation for the bemused congregation, who simply assume it is 'what the Vicar likes' – and too often that is indeed all it is. Confessional *prie-dieux* languish unused in dusty corners. The Eucharist may have its central place, but what it is about remains a total mystery to many – in the wrong as well as in the right sense. In addition to making our churches more user-friendly, if we want them to grow we also need to make them more visitor-friendly. We forget the oppressive fear that churches inspire in very many who are unused to them: not least the terror of 'being shown up' and 'doing the wrong thing'. (Witness the nervous hovering of the majority at the church door at a baptism or wedding before entering at the last possible moment; and the hunted look in their eyes when they do.) Once recognized, these fears can be addressed by a careful, unpatronizing policy of welcoming and helping.

There is a hunger for Catholic spirituality. Some who have come to church for years need the simplest teaching about how to start praying. Others need to move on, to hear about meditation, the daily office, spiritual direction, retreats, pilgrimages, devotion to the saints. Every Anglican should know, and should have visited, one of our religious communities (George Carey called them 'the best-kept secret in Anglicanism');[14] and many would profit from becoming tertiaries or oblates. At the Eucharist all too often a superficial vision of the Vatican II reforms has been allowed to undermine an atmosphere of prayerfulness. There are certainly good reasons for the priest to face the people, for standing instead of kneeling, and for the increased chumminess of liturgy and music; but they can also militate against any sense of the numinous. The awe, the sense of the beyond, the mystery of making the eternal present, the 'beauty of holiness' which characterized the older ritual and language have been widely lost in parish churches. Certainly there are gains in terms of intelligibility and in expressing the 'horizontal' dimension of the Eucharist, and I am not suggesting we should turn back; but we do need to consider how we can make good what has been lost and feed people's hunger for the transcendent. It is hardly surprising if they turn to the dubious mysticisms of the New Age if we keep them ignorant of the spiritual depths and treasures of our own tradition, and if our worship is human-centred, trite and banal.

There is a hunger for honest moral guidance; one which informs the conscience, avoids the easy answers of Catholic or Protestant fundamentalism, and acknowledges the demands of corporate as well as individual morality. In face of the complexities of contemporary decision-making in our social and personal life, and despite the media's caricatures of Anglican indecisiveness, we should be proud, not ashamed, of a Church which has the courage to conduct moral debate in public and to treat its members as adults. What matters is that all the church's members are equipped with the teaching and tools necessary for making responsible choices in the light of the Gospel. In the age of the sound bite and the one-line answer, Catholics need to witness the *whole* truth about the *whole* person and the *whole* of society. And against the popular perception of Anglican 'wetness' let's affirm loudly that no genuine Catholic church ought to be a 'kicking out' kind of church. If we give shelter to the others' refugees and casualties, that too is a cause of pride, not shame; not a sign of lax moral standards, but the exercise of Christ's standard of welcoming and loving people first, not waiting until in our opinion they have made themselves worthy of him.

There is a hunger for healing. The sacrament of anointing the sick, used publicly or privately, is thankfully returning to the Church's consciousness, and in not a few Evangelical parishes too. Without falling into dangerous naiveties, we are learning again to *expect* Christ to heal us and make us whole through the ministry of the Church. The sacrament of reconciliation – confession – on the other hand, remains Anglicanism's second best-kept secret, and badly needs resurrection from the dead. It is no use Catholic priests arguing in Synod for the right to say 'I absolve you', if no one sees the use of confessing their sins anyway. Somehow we have to get over the Dave Allen-type caricature of confession which has made it ridiculous in popular perception. As John Davies argues,[15] Catholic clergy too often in the past presented confession as a mechanical discipline, and too rarely as the invaluable aid that it is to healing and personal growth. We need priests who are properly trained to be wise confessors, and new ways of presenting the sacrament that are accessible and non-threatening. (Here too we have something to learn from post-Vatican II developments in the Roman Catholic Church's understanding and practice.) Confession is something we must be seen to be offering, seriously and professionally, because, as any therapist or GP will agree, there are millions of people burdened with guilt who need nothing so much as to hear the words 'I absolve you'. To be able to say with authority, 'You are forgiven, you are wanted, you are loved; now go and *live*' – that is an enormously healing thing, a gift which no one but the Church can give.

A reasoning Faith
All these hungers clamouring within the Church give us an agenda for Affirming Catholicism, in keeping with our stated aim to 'teach the Catholic faith' in a way that can be heard today. It might be objected that this is to put too much emphasis on education in a rather elitist way; Affirming Catholicism has regularly come under attack for its comfortable, liberal intellectual ethos. That is certainly not a problem we can ignore; we share it with most of the Anglican church in Britain, which is overwhelmingly a society of educated, middle-class people. But there is no avoiding the truth that at any intellectual level of development, from nursery infant to university professor, our understanding and teaching of the faith must be squared with our reason. Otherwise faith itself will falter and fail, and will ultimately be sloughed off as something that no longer fits our experience.

Hooker is probably Anglicanism's foremost champion of reason, and argu-ably the principal architect of the Anglican theological tradition. His best-known contribution was to describe our authoritative sources of Christian truth as 'a threefold chord, not quickly broken' – of scripture, tradition and reason. God's own nature is eternal reason; and our capacity to reason is a major aspect of our being made in God's image. It is only by the power of reason, as well as by prayer and the Spirit, that we are able to interpret and apply scripture to present circumstances, and it is through this continuing dialogue of reason, scripture, past teaching and new experience that tradition itself must constantly evolve. Much has been said and written in Affirming Catholicism about the evolutionary nature of a genuinely Catholic tradition. Point 4 of our original statement of aims reads: 'We affirm that Catholic tradition is not a static but a living thing, rooted in the revelation of Jesus Christ and growing in the experience of the Church.' What we stand for is an intelligent traditionalism which keeps faith and continuity with its Catholic inheritance, but rejects the reactionary view of tradition which has misunderstood tradition's own nature by regarding it as a closed body of received doctrine and practice. In Rowan Williams' telling observation, a genuine Catholicism trains its own critics – and so remains able to speak meaningfully to the world.

Among the marks of Anglo-Catholic decline in recent years have been an increasingly fundamentalist, anti-intellectual stance and the disappearance of academically respectable leadership; while at the parish level a paternalistic 'Father knows best' attitude on the part of the clergy will simply no longer wash. People require explanations, and in a more questioning age it can all too quickly become clear that Father probably does not know best – indeed may not know very much at all. We do not need less Christian education – we need far more, and far better, for everyone, at every level. The important thing is that it should be done in a way which effectively addresses people where they are. Affirming Catholicism is relatively rich in people who are able to deploy intellectual argument. The weakness we share with the rest of our Church is that we have hardly come to grips with the problem of communicating at a more popular level: which means not only simpler publications, but increasingly the use of non-literary information media. Unless we do, we seem likely to remain as bad as we now are at attracting, holding and teaching those who do not fall into the 'educated middle class' category.

Catholic social awareness

This brings us to social issues. Anglo-Catholics have prided themselves on a distinguished tradition of social conscience and social service, if not of socialism itself. We can point to the slum priests of the East End: F D Maurice; Conrad Noel; William Temple; Frank Weston and his famous dictum that 'you cannot worship Jesus in the tabernacle if you do not pity him in the slum'; and a host of Catholic societies from the Guild of St Matthew and the Christian Social Union up to the Jubilee Group in the present day. It is an impressive inheritance, though Ken Leech and others have exploded the notion that the Catholic movement was ever chiefly or even widely characterized by a strong social or socialist awareness.[16] Relatively speaking, it is probably fair to say that the incarnational and sacramental emphasis of Catholicism, with its instinctive refusal to draw a clear boundary between the Church and the world, has tended to lead naturally to a greater involvement *in* the world and in social concerns; while the classic Protestant emphasis on the Atonement and justification by faith tended to stress individual piety and salvation *from* the world. On the other hand, in recent years at least on the British scene, it is also fair to say that while Evangelical concern with social and political issues has shown a marked increase, visible Anglo-Catholic concern for social justice, with the honourable exception of the Jubilee Group, has dwindled almost to vanishing point. This is despite the sharpening division of wealth in our society since the eighties, along with the increase of unemployment, racial violence and homelessness. As Leech remarks, Anglo-Catholicism seems to have entirely diverted its attention from these things to its own internal pathologies.

What might be a specifically Catholic contribution to contemporary social thinking?
Perhaps partly because of the traditional incarnational analogy with God's involvement in the material world, Anglo-Catholic social concern, typified in the slum priest, was frequently more condescending and paternalistic in character than genuinely socialist or egalitarian. Ken Leech notes a related danger for the Church today, which like other charitable agencies is increasingly expected to help alleviate the results of social distress, but also increasingly condemned when it questions the causes of that distress. (The dilemma is summed up in the words of Bishop Helder Camara: 'When I gave bread to the poor they called me a saint. When I asked why the poor had no bread, they called me a Communist'.) Paternalistic charity not only provides no more than a short-term palliative, it can reinforce an unjust system by masking its worst results. In an important contribution to our first conference Alan Billings[17] suggested, following others like Leech and Noel, that instead of the incarnational model, the model of the Trinity, which reminds us that personhood, though free and individual, nevertheless exists only in relation to other persons, may be a better corrective to the market-driven individualism of contemporary Britain. We have learned the dangers of state collectivism from the collapsed Communist regimes; and we have also learned that even social organisations set up for the welfare of individuals can also end up disempowering them in a 'dependency culture'. What we need is a more nuanced social morality and practice – one, in fact, which reflects precisely the paradox of the Trinity: that personal freedom and personal community are correlatives, not opposites. A trinitarian understanding of

personhood nails the lie that 'there is no such thing as society, only individuals'. Respect for the individual entails responsibility for the individuals; and individuals can only be integrated healthy persons when in responsible relation to others.

On a broader canvas, 'postmodernist' writers have also characterized the current state of Western civilization by its individualism, pluralism of values and loss of any commonly accepted meaning. In art and popular music postmodernism is expressed in collage and montage; everything is a collection of bits and pieces whose meaning arises only from what they are. In literature it is represented by 'deconstructionism' which refuses any connection between author and text, between signifiers and what is signified. In the media it is represented by the shift from a verbal culture to an image culture, typified in the video screen, the TV 'channel surfer', video games and systems of 'virtual reality' which seal the subject into enjoyment of a private world. More hopefully however (as Angela Tilby has explained for us[18]) postmodern science seems to be moving in the opposite direction. Work on chaos theory and 'complexity' is focusing on whole systems, on interconnectedness; contemporary cosmology has suggested the 'anthropic principle', a sign of organic causation in the universe that seems geared to the evolution of the personal.

As the term postmodernism itself implies, the loss of a uniting idea or goal is attributed not to the loss of God, but to the loss of a naive 'modernist' faith in human power alone to create real progress. David Lyon sees in this a ray of hope:

> Once, the idea that the future is in human hands was confidently asserted. This modern arrogance denied the divine and diverted all hope to human resources. Today the human is being displaced, decentred, and the grip on the future seems once more up for grabs. While this opens the door to everything from Foucault's play of power to the Age of Aquarius, it also renders more plausible the possibility that Providence was not such a bad idea after all. Perhaps postmodern apocalyptics will have to make space for a vision of a new earth, that antique agent of social change, and the original partner of final judgment.[19]

If we accept the postmodern analysis of where we are now, it poses very clear challenges for the Church. In an essay on religion and postmodernism entitled 'The Ash Tray of Modernity' David Atkinson sets them out:

> Part of the mission of the Christian Church is to be a bearer of meaning, significance and hope. Do we do this through Christian presence, Christian action, Christian proclamation? I am sure it has to do with the whole task, in which all these elements of mission belong together: worship, apologetics, religious experience, demonstrated love, social justice, the creation of community, the recovery of the capacity for commitment. If the Church can find such ways of being the Church in a post-

modern world, maybe these are phoenix-figures which could rise out of the ashes – or perhaps resurrections from the dead.[20]

What specifically does an Affirming Catholic faith have to offer? In the new spiritual market place we can affirm the most ancient, continuous and best-attested brand on offer; yet unlike its more fundamentalist alternatives we can also affirm human reason, personal freedom and the evolving nature of our own tradition; and unlike the escapist gnosticisms of the New Age we also affirm the world, our involvement in it and our responsibilities for one another. In face of prevailing meaninglessness we have a plain meaning to supply: a God who made the universe and us for himself, who sent his Son to heal our lostness and reunite us with him, and who unites himself to us still, physically and spiritually, in prayer, word and sacrament. In the face of plural moralities and uncommitted individualisms we know we are called to be one Body, with a morality of practical love whose social expression is care for others and the fight for justice. In the face of ecological and environmental menaces we affirm the goodness of creation, our responsibility as its stewards, and God's continuing involvement in the world he gave us. And in the face of disconnectedness, alienation and death we affirm that the ground of our existence is an eternal, personal Love who has called forth other persons of supreme value – us – and created us for loving communion with one another and with him, for ever.

Postscript

I have tried to say what Affirming Catholicism is for, and to outline some of the particular gifts and insights we have to offer the Church and the world. But there is more to say. Let me return to the start and explain what drew me to Catholicism in the first place.

The first thing was the sheer power of Catholic worship. After worshipping for years in a whitewashed box, where the only form of warmth and beauty on offer was in the hymn singing, Catholic liturgy struck me immediately as a riot of sense impressions: the music, the colour of the vestments, the sight and smell of incense, the flickering candles, the solemn dance of ritual. It was a symphony of the senses somehow expressing something tremendous: a vision of the glory of God, the eternal made tangible in the present. The first time I attended a High Mass I remember having to struggle to suppress laughter, not out of amusement, and certainly not mockery, but for sheer joy. I *felt* it when the priest sang 'With angels and archangels and the whole company of heaven'. Time stopped, and the barriers were down; and when later I found Keble's poem on the Mass, I recognized not just the image, but the experience:

> What is this silent might, making our darkness light,
> New wine our water, heavenly blood our wine?
> Christ, and his Mother dear, and all his saints, are here;
> And where they are is heaven; and what they touch, divine.

The second thing, oddly allied to this vision of holiness, was the realization that Catholicism was fun. Here were priests and sincere worshippers who drank and swore and went to the pub after Mass. There was no mask of piety of moralism. It might have shocked some of my family, but it certainly pleased me. At about that time I came across a line, I think, of Michael Marshall's, 'The test of Catholic Christianity is not so much whether it can make good men better, but whether it can make bad men holy'. I began to see that real holiness really is about wholeness. God doesn't make us holy by asking us to suppress and cut away parts of us, but by recreating and restoring us to be more fully and truly ourselves. The Church is Catholic, inclusive, because God is Catholic, inclusive. He takes all of us and every part of us as we are, then *loves* us back into the people he wants us to be. This understanding puts sin in perspective, as something God can still turn to the good (though my Calvinist depths still struggle to accept it). As

Augustine said, 'Even sin has its uses, if sin makes us fall back on God'. That is not to say Catholicism doesn't take sin seriously, but it will never allow it to conquer joy. I understood why the Church is able to talk about *celebrating* the sacrament of reconciliation.

A third discovery was the Catholic doctrine of the Atonement, which had a particular importance for me. The explanation of the Cross that I had been given went like this. 'God was very angry with us for our sins, and as a matter of justice had condemned us all to death. But then he sent his Son to suffer and die for us instead, and because Jesus was sinless God substitutes his punishment for the one due to us. Jesus took the rap, and we got let off provided we promised to be good.' It is a terrible explanation, as illogical as it is barbarous, and it tends to lodge a monstrous picture of God in the mind forever after. Alas, it is still very commonly taught. The Catholic faith assured me, with St Paul, that 'God was *in* Christ reconciling the world to himself' – not far away subjecting him to substitutionary tortures. I understood that the Cross is all of a piece with the Incarnation. Because God is Love, he did what love does; he strove to unite himself with the beloved. God became man in Christ to identify himself with us, to put himself where we are. The cross and death of Christ are the ultimate point of that identification with us. He shares completely in our lostness, our suffering and finally our death, so that through death we can come to share in his resurrection.

I came to understand too that Christ's death and resurrection are not only historical fact but also eternal process. We are united with him in baptism and made part of his Body, so that the Christian life itself is a continuing cycle, dying daily and rising with Christ, gradually losing an old self to be made a new self in him. This is the mystery made present and real for us now, in its continuing aspect especially in the Eucharist, so that we are drawn into it and made part of it ourselves, and can understand our own sufferings and victories as a sharing in his. These are profound truths of Catholic (and of course New Testament) doctrine which are too seldom spoken of in teaching and preaching; but they are also the stuff of experience, the pattern and context of the spiritual life.

Mary and the saints became important to me. I had always understood that the Christian faith consists in a restored relationship with God our Father, but I had not understood that this naturally brings us into a network of eternal relationships with the whole family of God, visible and invisible. Perhaps the liturgical breaking of the barriers of time and space awoke in me some instinctive Celtic awareness of the other world; but it has always seemed natural to me that Christians who believe in the mystical Body should communicate with its other members. What is the Communion of Saints if there is no communication with them? The Catholic faith teaches us to understand that the saints pray and care for us, and it teaches us to pray for the dead, because of course they are not dead; we are still one Body, and they like us are continuing to grow to their completion in the love of God. We have 'friends on earth and friends above'; and mutual prayer for each other is the way we express our unity and love, whether we happen to be here or there.

Last year I took a joint pilgrimage of my own parishioners and Westcott House students to the shrine of Our Lady at Walsingham. Most of them had never been there before, and were not exactly, what might be called card-carrying Catholics. I had qualms about going because Walsingham had declared itself for the time being a no-go area for women priests, and several of the students were women ordinands. They were suspicious of the place, as perhaps many Affirming Catholics would be suspicious too. Anyway we went. My brief was to explain the place, to translate it and make it real for them. I was more than glad to do it. I love Walsingham. In a more than worldly sense I have felt at home there. I love it because it stands for an uncompromising Catholic faith which is warm and exuberant and frankly vulgar, but at least it isn't afraid of showing devotion and emotion. Of course, it is full of flaws and all the old pathologies of Anglo-Catholicism, but it still has enormous depth and warmth and converting power, and, let it be said, it is one place which does attract categories other than the educated middle class. It is what the Irish call a 'thin' place between heaven and earth, a place where the doctrine of the Communion of Saints comes alive, where devotion to Mary becomes something warm and real instead of being just a party badge. It is a sacramental place; there is a sense of Christ incarnate in the Mass and incarnate in your friends drinking at the Bull. Anyway, it worked. Unlikely fodder as they were, I could see the place working on them as it began to work on me years ago. They found something that got them in the guts; and they wanted to go back. They had found the thing that the Catholic movement was always supposed to be about.

I hope Affirming Catholicism will never become so respectable that we will be prepared to lose any of this. Certainly a lot needs explaining, translating, re-expressing and making accessible to the present day; and that is precisely what we are for. In this movement we have written and talked a great deal about the inherently evolving nature of genuine Catholic tradition; and ours is the task of responsibly assisting the evolution. Forgive me if I repeat something I wrote elsewhere:

> Our answer to the sort of rhetoric that talks airily about the end of the Catholic movement in the Anglican Church is that *we are* the Catholic movement in the Church now. What that means is that we have to do the serious theological and spiritual work of assisting the evolution from within, helping people to see that change can be truly a fulfilment and not an abolition. But to save Anglican Catholicism we will have to be in it heart and soul, and graciously in it. We have to allay

people's fears; we have to keep driving the message that real Catholicism is both changing and continuous; and above all we have to be active reconcilers now. There are thousands of loyal Catholics who have been told again and again that their faith is finished in the 'C of E'. They feel confused and stranded, and it is up to us to give them a home, or rather to help them see they still belong in the home they have, and that not one jot or tittle of our Catholic heritage has passed away. Many – probably most – 'unaffirming' Catholics are unhappy in their new isolation, uninterested in Rome, and looking for a way to change without loss of face or integrity. For their sake and ours we should be looking for ways to keep communicating across the barriers. But we shall not convince anyone unless our own commitment to the Catholic faith is clear, and we are rooted and grounded in God and the inheritance he has given us.

Certainly there is plenty that has been wrong in Anglo-Catholicism, but enough has been said about it. It is time to say that there is plenty more that remains true and powerful and profound and holy, and it is not to be hived off from our church, whether to Rome or up some blind alley of 'alternative oversight'. As I write, I have heard the heartening news that the leading Catholic theological college in the Church of England, St Stephen's House, Oxford, is to admit women to train for the priesthood, and to allow women priests to celebrate Mass there. That is a significant change, and a cause for rejoicing. The barriers *will* come down, and the hurts will heal. Let's look forward to the first woman celebrant at Walsingham, and at all the places where the 'full faith' has been faithfully proclaimed. And let's pray and work for the day when the Anglican Church, and the whole Church, will be fully Catholic, Evangelical, Affirming, and One.

Notes

1   W. S. F. Pickering, *Anglo-Catholicism: A Study in Religious Ambiguity* (SPCK 1989) p. 143

2   V. Strudwick, *Is the Anglican Church Catholic?: The Catholicity of Anglicanism* (DLT – Affirming Catholicism 1994)·

3   J. Habgood, 'Catholicity' in *Making Sense* (SPCK 1993) p. 157

4   *Ibid.*

5   *Unitatis Redintegratio* para 22

6   *Ibid.* para 3

7   S. Sykes, 'Foundations of an Anglican Ecclesiology' in *Living the Mystery: Affirming Catholicism and the Future of Anglicanism* (ed. J. John) (DLT 1994)
P. Avis, 'Towards an Authentic Paradigm for Anglicanism' in *Anglicanism and the Christian Church* (T & T Clark 1989)

8   H. Montefiore, 'The Historic Episcopate' in *The Historic Episcopate* (ed. K. Carey) (Dacre 1954)

9   P. Avis, *Anglicanism and the Christian Church* (note 7) p. 309

10   J. Halliburton, 'Orders and Ordination' in *Together in Mission and Ministry* (Church House 1993) p. 164

11   See J. Sedgwick, *Why Women Priests? The ordination of Women and the Apostolic Ministry* (DLT – Affirming Catholicism 1993)

12   Quoted by Strudwick (note 2) p. 21

13   G. Carey, 'Revitalizing the Catholic tradition' in *Living Tradition: Affirming Catholicism in the Anglican Church* (ed. J. John) (DLT 1992) p. 18

14   *Ibid.* p. 26

15   J. Davies, *Affirming Confession* (DLT – Affirming Catholicism 1995)

[16] K. Leech, *Politics and the Faith Today: Catholic Social Vision for the 1990s* (DLT – Affirming Catholicism 1994)

[17] A. Billings, 'What Sort of Society Are We Envisaging Now' in *Living Tradition* (note 13)

[18] A. Tilby, 'Holy Stardust' in *Living the Mystery* (note 7)

[19] D. Lyon, *Postmodernity* (Open University Press 1994) p. 86

[20] D. Atkinson (unpublished discussion paper 1995)

Other booklets in the Affirming Catholicism series